romans

A DOUBLE-EDGED BIBLE STUDY

TH1NK: **Life**Change™

TH1NK
P.O. Box 35001
Colorado Springs, Colorado 80935

www.navpress.com

TH1NK is an imprint of NavPress.

TH1NK and the TH1NK logo are registered trademarks of NavPress. Absence of ® in connection with marks of NavPress or other parties does not indicate an absence of registration of those marks.

ISBN 1-57683-850-1

Cover design by Arvid Wallen

Creative Team: Gabe Filkey s.c.m., Nicci Jordan, Melanie Knox, Steve Parolini, Arvid Wallen, Kathy Mosier, Glynese Northam

Printed in Canada

2 3 4 5 6 7 8 9 10 / 09 08 07 06 05

contents

introduction to
TH1NK: LifeChange

Double-Edged and Ready for Action

For the word of God is living and active. Sharper than any double-edged sword, it penetrates even to dividing soul and spirit, joints and marrow; it judges the thoughts and attitudes of the heart.

Hebrews 4:12

a reason to study

Studying the Bible is more than homework. It is more than reading a textbook. And it is more than an opportunity for a social gathering. Like Hebrews suggests, the Bible knows us, challenges us, and, yes, judges us. Like a double-edged sword, it's sharp enough to cut through our layers of insecurity and pretense to change our lives forever.

Deep down, isn't that what we want–to actually *experience* God's power in our lives through Scripture? That's what TH1NK: LifeChange is all about. The purpose of this Bible study is to connect you intimately with God's Word. It can change you, not only intellectually but also spiritually, emotionally, maybe even physically. God's Word is that powerful.

The psalmist wrote,

> *What you say goes, GOD,*
> *and stays, as permanent as the heavens.*
> *Your truth never goes out of fashion;*
> *it's as up-to-date as the earth when the sun comes*
> *up. . . .*
> *If your revelation hadn't delighted me so,*
> *I would have given up when the hard times came.*
> *But I'll never forget the advice you gave me;*
> *you saved my life with those wise words.*
> *Save me! I'm all yours.*
> *I look high and low for your words of wisdom.*
> *The wicked lie in ambush to destroy me,*
> *but I'm only concerned with your plans for me.*
> *I see the limits to everything human,*
> *but the horizons can't contain your commands!*
> (PSALM 119:89-90,92-96, MSG)

Do you notice the intimate connection the psalmist has with God *because* of the greatness of the Word? He trusts God, he loves Him, and his greatest desire is to obey Him. But the only way he knows how to do any of this is because he knows God's voice, God's words.

the details

Each TH1NK: LifeChange study covers one book of the Bible so you can concentrate on its particular, essential details. Although every study covers a different book, there are common threads throughout the series. Each study will do the following:

1. Help you understand the book you're studying so well that it affects your daily thinking
2. Teach valuable Bible study skills you can use on your own to go even deeper into God's Word
3. Provide a contextual understanding of the book, offering historical background, word definitions, and explanatory notes
4. Allow you to understand the message of the book as a whole
5. Demonstrate how God's Word can transform you into a bona fide representative of Jesus

Every week, plan on spending about thirty to forty-five minutes on your own to complete the study. Then get together with your group. Depending on the amount of time it takes, you can either go through a whole or a half lesson each week. If you do one lesson per week, you'll finish the study in just under three months. But it's all up to you.

the structure

The eleven lessons include the following elements:

Study. First you'll study the book by yourself. This is where you'll answer questions, learn cultural and biographical information, and ask God some questions of your own.

Live. After you've absorbed the information, you'll want to look in a mirror—figuratively, that is. Think about your life in the context of what you've learned. This is a time to be honest with yourself and with God about who you are and how you are living.

Connect. You know that a small-group study time isn't just for hanging out and drinking soda. A small group provides accountability and support. It's one thing to say to yourself, *I'm really going to work on this* and entirely another thing to say it to a group of your friends. Your friends can support your decisions, encourage you to follow through, and pray for you regularly. And vice versa.

In your group, you'll want to talk with each other about what you discovered on your own, things that went unanswered, things that challenged you, and things that changed you. Use the guidance in this section to lead your discussion. After that, pray for each other.

Go deeper. Thirsty for more? Just can't get enough? Then use the guidance in this section to explore even deeper the vastness of Scripture. It's similar to extra credit for all you overachievers who love to learn.

Memory verse of the week. Did a particular verse make you think? Is there a verse you can't get out of your head? Write it down and memorize it. Allow God's Word to permanently brand itself in your head and your heart.

Notes. At the end of each chapter, there are some pages for notes. Use them to ask questions of God or yourself, to write important verses and observations, or for anything else you want to jot down.

now go!

You are now ready to experience God and the Bible in an intense new way. So jump in headfirst. Allow the double-edged sword of Scripture to pierce your mind, your heart, your life.

Introduction to Romans

Christian living

Trying to live the Christian life without the Bible would be like trying to climb Mount Everest without any gear. Lots of New Testament letters address elements of the Christian life, such as love, sacrifice, the role of works versus faith, sin, law fulfillment, and so on. But none cover a broader gamut than Romans. This sixteen-chapter book answers many questions about the Christian life even before we ask them.

Not that Romans offers any formulas or easy answers. Quite the opposite. Reading Romans can be intense; it is easy to get lost in the wisdom, theology, and variety of topics. But at the same time, the knowledge it brings provides a solid foundation for asking questions of God and enduring this mountain climb called life. Without Romans, we'd be perpetual wanderers, clueless about how grace, justice, sin, and redemption interplay.

Romans encourages us, scares us, engages us, understands us, admonishes us, and gives us hope in Christ that transcends all other emotions. Within this book, we find so much hope, so much understanding and empathy. Paul has felt what we so often feel: tired, sinful, deflated, and confused.

As you study this book, the premier document of Christian theology, you'll have much to think about. Take as much time as you need to digest new ideas and to contemplate teachings that can be hard to swallow. But first, here's some background information that will help you in your study.

map of the Roman Empire

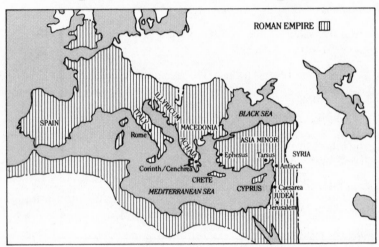

who is Saul, aka Paul?

If you were a Roman citizen reading this letter for the first time, you'd have a few preconceived notions about Saul (later known as Paul). He was born in the first decade after Christ's death in Tarsus, a wealthy city on the trade route from Syria to Asia Minor. Tarsus was known for its schools of philosophy and liberal arts, and Saul may have had some contact with them. Later on in one of his letters, he calls himself a "Hebrew of Hebrews" (Philippians 3:5), which probably means his parents spoke Hebrew and raised him in a strict Jewish home. They named him Saul after Israel's first king; their family belonged to King Saul's tribe of Benjamin. Saul's family was at least somewhat prosperous because he was not only a citizen of Tarsus but also a citizen of Rome.

Paul's ministry timeline

(All dates are approximate, based on F. F. Bruce, *Paul: Apostle of the Heart Set Free*, 475.)

Public ministry of Jesus	28–30 AD
Conversion of Paul (Acts 9:1-19)	33
Paul visits Jerusalem to see Peter (Galatians 1:18)	35
Paul in Cilicia and Syria (Galatians 1:21; Acts 9:30)	35–46
Paul visits Jerusalem to clarify the mission to the Gentiles (Galatians 2:1-10)	46
Paul and Barnabas in Cyprus and Galatia (Acts 13–14)	47–48
Letter to the Galatians	48?
Council of Jerusalem (Acts 15)	49
Paul and Silas travel from Antioch to Asia Minor, Macedonia, and Achaia (Acts 16–17)	49–50
Letters to the Thessalonians	50
Paul in Corinth (Acts 18:1-18)	50–52
Paul visits Jerusalem	52
Paul in Ephesus (Acts 19)	52–55
Letters to the Corinthians	55–56
Paul travels to Macedonia, Dalmatia, and Achaia (Acts 20)	55–57
Letter to the Romans	early 57
Paul to Jerusalem (Acts 21:1–23:22)	May 57
Paul imprisoned in Caesarea (Acts 23:23–26:32)	57–59
Paul sent to house arrest in Rome (Acts 27:1–28:31)	59–62
Letters to Philippians, Colossians, Ephesians, Philemon	60?–62
Letters to Timothy and Titus	?
Paul executed in Rome	65?

It's also evident that Saul came from a good family because he was sent to study Jewish Law in Jerusalem under the most popular rabbi of his day, the Pharisee Gamaliel. The Pharisees (which in Hebrew means "separated ones") felt God had set them apart to live by the Torah (the Law, or teaching, of Moses). For them, that meant following the Torah as interpreted by generations of Jewish teachers. Some Pharisees believed that a man was righteous if he did more good than bad, but Saul followed the stricter group that insisted that every tiny implication of the Law must be kept.

After Jesus died and some Jews chose to follow Him as the Messiah—and in doing so espoused totally unique interpretations of the Torah—the Pharisees, including Saul, were raging mad. Saul helped lead the fight in Jerusalem against those who proclaimed Christ. After driving many Christians out of Jerusalem, he got permission to kick more out of Damascus. But on the road to Damascus, Jesus confronted Saul by blinding him and revealing to him that he was persecuting the very God he claimed to worship. (It makes you wonder if Jesus still uses miraculous methods like that to get our attention. When was the last time you heard a story like Saul's?)

After that, Saul changed from a legalistic, stiff-necked, intolerant meanie to a devoted follower of Jesus Christ, the Messiah. The very passion that had fueled his hatred of Christ-followers now fueled his love for Christ. Saul joined the Jews who were urging other Jews to believe in Jesus, and soon God called him to take his message to the Gentiles (non-Jews) too. When he began working with the Gentiles, he took on the Greek name Paul so they would be able to relate better to him.

mission unstoppable

There was no stopping Paul once he met Christ. After his conversion, he immediately moved outward into pagan lands. Here's a brief summary of his travels: He spent seven years in Cilicia and Syria and then went with Barnabas to Syrian Antioch. By that time, the church had become more Gentile than Jewish.

Later, Paul and Barnabas went to Cyprus and Galatia for about two years. They then returned to Antioch, where some teachers of the Law claimed that Gentile Christians must be circumcised to follow Jewish Law. Paul and Barnabas strongly disagreed and eventually went to Jerusalem to have the apostles renounce the idea. The apostles agreed with Paul and Barnabas that Gentile Christians had to be moral and avoid idolatry but didn't have to keep Jewish customs. It's too bad this didn't just settle the matter. Paul struggled with this controversy for years.

After his time in Jerusalem, Paul launched another missionary campaign with Silas and some other friends. He spent four years in Asia, Macedonia, and Achaia (Greece). After a quick trip to Jerusalem and Antioch, he took a third trip to Ephesus and then finally to Corinth. (Do these names sound familiar?) In Corinth, he stayed with a friend named Gaius, and that's probably when he wrote this letter to the Romans. After he wrote the letter, he headed back to Jerusalem.

Roman holiday

Okay, so it wasn't quite a holiday. In fact, Paul's long-awaited visit to Rome didn't even remotely match his plans. Instead of spending long periods of time with his beloved Romans, he ended up in prison in Caesarea. He spent two years in prison because the Roman authorities were angry about his work in converting Gentiles, but when a new Roman governor suggested sending Paul to stand trial in a Jewish court, Paul appealed for a trial before Caesar.

It had to be frustrating for Paul, not only because he wanted to spend time with his Roman friends but also because it took him so long to actually get to Rome. It took almost a year because of a storm and shipwreck. He arrived about three years after he wrote this letter announcing his plan to visit.

why a letter?

By AD 57, Paul had already spent twenty years as a missionary. Now that local leaders were equipped to care for the churches Paul had planted, he decided he was going to head west to Spain, stopping first in Rome.

Although he was legally a citizen of Rome, Paul had never seen the famed capital of the empire. A stay there would be a chance to meet members of the church already flourishing in Rome. Paul hoped that the Roman Christians would help provide funds and a base of operations for his mission to Spain.

But a few factors held up his visit, so he wrote a letter. Why a letter? Well, in the first place, he knew only a few Christians (out of the hundreds) who lived in Rome. It may seem surprising, then, that in the introduction to Romans, Paul wrote with such affection toward them. But in Paul's time, written greetings were all very similar to this (although he added a Christian spin to his). And while Paul had a soft spot for the Christians he *did* know in Rome, he also felt an honor and respect for the great and powerful Rome. Before he could ask the Christians there for money to support his missionary travels and then set up shop in their home, he needed to tell them who he was and what he was about. Second, Paul had collected money for the poor Christians in Jerusalem and felt it was his duty to stop there first. So he wrote this letter to prepare the Romans for his visit—a letter that just happened to become his greatest treatise on the gospel.

the big picture

For the wages of sin is death, but the gift of God is eternal life in Christ Jesus our Lord.

Romans 6:23

It would be difficult to study individual parts of a painting by Picasso without having seen the entire work. Can you imagine being asked to answer questions such as "What was Picasso communicating through his *Two Women Running on the Beach?*" when all you can see is the section showing a foot, or "How would you analyze his blue period?" when all you're given is a scrap of a blue painting? It would be a frustrating exercise because although you could make assumptions based on pieces of the paintings, you still wouldn't have the big picture.

Similarly, the first thing you've got to do before studying the book of Romans is read it–the whole thing. Like analyzing Picasso's art, unless you've experienced the entire work, your attempts to study the book will be frustrating at best.

It may take you a while to get through all sixteen chapters of Romans, so this first lesson is devoted entirely to that objective. You'll have opportunities to make comments as you read, but just concentrate on getting through the book. If you're feeling particularly ambitious, read it in a couple of different translations. Try, perhaps, the NIV (*New International Version*) and then *The Message.* That way, you'll connect with both the *meanings* and the *feelings* of the text.

Read Paul's letter to the Romans.

1 As you read, write down your first impressions of the book. Consider the following questions and take notes in the space that follows each.

a What themes show up? Do you notice one unifying topic throughout the book?

b What is Paul's tone? Is he friendly, compassionate, funny, dry?

c What words does Paul repeat? (Repetition often clues us in to the author's focus.)

d What kinds of language does Paul use? Metaphors and pictures? Stories? Commands?

2 How does your first reading of Romans affect your ideas about God?

3 If you haven't already, read the introduction on pages 11–16. This will further acquaint you with Romans and show you how the book fits in with God's great gospel.

live

4 As you read the book of Romans, what affected you most? Did anything speak to a current issue in your life or to any theological struggles you may be working through? Did it help you with these issues or confuse you?

5 What questions have been prompted by your reading?

6 Write down any goals you have for your study of Romans.

connect

Talk with your group about your hopes and expectations for this study. Have someone write them down so that as you go through the study, your leader can remind you of your goals and help you hold each other accountable. Then pray together, asking God to lead your group to a deeper understanding of Him through this incredible, critical book of Scripture.

go deeper

Paul carefully organized his message to the Romans. Observe the natural breaks in his thoughts and make an outline based on what you discover. Then write a short summary for each division.

Here are the divisions the NIV suggests, but you can divide the
book differently if you'd like:

1:1-7	4:1-25	8:18-27	12:1-8
1:8-17	5:1-11	8:28-39	12:9-21
1:18-32	5:12-21	9:1-29	13:1-7
2:1-16	6:1-14	9:30–10:21	13:8-14
2:17-29	6:15-23	11:1-10	14:1–15:13
3:1-8	7:1-6	11:11-24	15:14-22
3:9-20	7:7-25	11:25-32	15:23-33
3:21-31	8:1-17	11:33-36	16:1-27

memory verse of the week 🎧

Did a particular verse make you think? Is there a verse you can't get out of your head? Write it down and memorize it. Allow God's Word to permanently brand itself in your head and your heart.

notes from group discussion

good news and bad news

I am not ashamed of the gospel, because it is the power of God for the salvation of everyone who believes.

Romans 1:16

"Do you want the good news or the bad news first?" Your answer to that familiar question can tell a lot about you. If you answer, "The good news," it may be because you feel you could better handle the blow of the bad news after you've been encouraged by the good. If you answer, "The bad news," perhaps you want to be let down first and then pleasantly surprised. In the first chapter of Romans, Paul doesn't offer a choice. He showers his readers with the good news and then hits them hard with the not-so-good.

When you start to read the chapter, you immediately feel encouraged and loved by Paul (even if you're not a Roman citizen). He thanks God for you, prays for you, tells you about grace and salvation, and then, just as you're really feeling good, he reminds you of the degenerate generation in which you live, a generation of people who've fallen into the deepest pits of humanity.

As you read, think about how this chapter relates to our culture today.

Read Romans 1.

The Good News: 1:1-17

• *Servant (1:1).* In the Old Testament, a servant of God
was a high official in the Lord's royal administration—think
Moses, Samuel, and David. To Gentiles, a servant was something
very different; he was either a free man who chose to work for his
master or a slave who had no choice but to serve his master. Paul
was aware of both these meanings when he used that specific word.

• *Apostle (1:1).* Apostle literally means "one who is sent," a messen-
ger. In Jewish Law, this was the *shaliach*, "a person acting with full
authority for another" in a business or legal transaction.[1] The early
church called those who had seen the risen Jesus "apostles." They
were the leaders regarded with authority over doctrine and policy.

1 Paul went beyond the customary greeting to tell more about
himself and his mission to people who didn't know him. In 1:1-7,
how did Paul identify the following?

Himself

His message

28

His mission

His readers

• *Obedience that comes from faith (1:5).* Some people think Paul meant the practical obedience that comes from believing in Jesus, while other interpreters think he meant that faith itself, rather than law-keeping, is the kind of obedience God desires.[2]

• *Saints (1:7).* Saint, sanctify, and holiness all explain the same Greek word-group that means "set apart." So, a saint is someone set apart by God who is already in the process of being made holy by the Holy Spirit.

• *Grace (1:5,7).* God's grace to us means that He gives us undeserved favor and gifts. Later in Romans, Paul talks a lot about what it means to receive God's grace through Jesus Christ. But here, he is talking about how simply amazing it is that God allows us to live the Christian life and fulfill our calls from Him.

2 Just like the Romans, we have been called to be obedient and to be saints. Consider what this means. How does this knowledge affect your actions, decisions, and priorities?

3   Why was Paul unashamed to preach the gospel, even among strangers in a sophisticated city like Rome or a foreign country like Spain (see 1:16)? In light of this, are you similar to or different from Paul?

Righteousness (1:17). To be righteous literally means to be in the right or declared not guilty. It's a legal term that Paul turned into a spiritual word to mean right with God.

fyi

4   How does the gospel enable people to be saved? What does "The righteous will live by faith" mean (1:17)?

5   Pay attention to Paul's attitudes, priorities, and desires in 1:1-17. How are they good examples for you to follow?

The Not-So-Good News: 1:18-32

6 What is Paul's main point in 1:18-32?

7 Paul says that man's wickedness suppresses the truth (see 1:18).

    a What truth do people suppress?

    b How do they suppress that truth?

8 Why would someone think that the knowledge of God is not worthwhile (see 1:28)?

9 Why does God give people over to depraved minds and actions (see 1:24,26,28)?

a In view of 1:21-23,28, why is that just?

b How could this "giving over" be a loving act on God's part?

> live

10 Look back at question 2. After considering your answer to that question, think of one specific way you can act in the obedience of faith (because you are righteous by faith and living by faith).

11 Does Paul's list of vices in 1:24-32 suggest any areas in which you need to repent? Consider envy, greed, deceit, boastfulness, disobedience, and so on.

connect

In your group, discuss the idea of faith. What do you think faith means? In what sense is faith itself an aspect of obedience? How does true faith also lead to obedience? Discuss any implications this might have on your lives and pray for each other that you would live lives of obedient faith in Christ.

The words *call* and *called* appear four times in 1:1-7. Who calls? Who is called? What are they called to be and do? After you've thought about these questions, think about your own calling. What have you been "set apart" to be and do?

memory verse of the week

Did a particular verse make you think? Is there a verse you can't get out of your head? Write it down and memorize it. Allow God's Word to permanently brand itself in your head and your heart.

notes from group discussion

the blame game

You, therefore, have no excuse, you who pass judgment on someone else, for at whatever point you judge the other, you are condemning yourself, because you who pass judgment do the same things.

Romans 2:1

We're pretty good at pointing fingers. Think about it. When someone does something stupid, we point and laugh. Maybe a friend slips on a wet floor. Or someone yells out an embarrassingly wrong answer in class. We also point and sneer. A friend goes too far with a boyfriend, and we look at her from our holier-than-thou perches with equal measures of disdain and judgment.

Romans 1 makes us want to point our fingers all over the place. "Hey, you people! Can't you get it right?!" But the next two chapters state that if we're going to point fingers, we should point only at ourselves.

Jesus doesn't point fingers at anyone. As it says in *The Message*, "We're sinners, every one of us, in the same sinking boat with everybody else . . . [and] out of sheer generosity he put us in right standing with himself" (Romans 3:19,24). Jesus doesn't expect any of us to be better than the next; He's smarter than that, and that's why He defeated sin for each and every one of us.

Read Romans 2–3.

study

• **Pass judgment (2:1).** Jesus and Paul both urge Christians
to pay attention when someone's teaching or behavior is
fyi
ungodly. If we notice something wrong, it might be appropriate to
speak to that person about the situation. But it may not. We have to
pray about it, confess any feelings of self-righteousness, condescen-
sion, or superiority we may have, and seek God's wisdom about a
possible confrontation.

• **Law (2:12).** This refers to the Law of Moses. Most Jews were
proud of knowing God's Word backward and forward and despised
Gentiles who didn't know it. Many Jews believed God would give
them eternal life just because they were born into Jewish families or
because they knew God's Word. It wasn't easy for Jews and Gentiles
to get over their prejudices toward each other, even after they
became Christians.

1 From your initial reading, what do you think Paul's main point is
in 2:1-16?

2 Why should you not judge other people's sin?

3 Give some more thought to the Jew versus Gentile debate.

> **a** Why did some Jews believe God considered them superior to the Gentiles (see 2:17-20)?

> **b** What argument was used to illustrate that the Jews were not superior to the Gentiles (see 2:21-24)?

> **c** Do you know any Christians (including yourself) who embody this description of the Jews? How can this passage shape your actions, words, and thoughts?

fyi *Circumcision (2:25).* This is a ritual cutting away of the foreskin, which signified that a man was a Jew. It was supposed to demonstrate that a man had committed to obeying the Lord, and it was a way of inviting God to cut off the man and his heirs if he rebelled against God.[1] But many of the Jews took it a step further and thought that circumcision meant guaranteed membership among God's people (even though Moses had warned Israel that the ritual was meaningless unless it was accompanied by "circumcision of the heart").

4 We know now not to boast in our knowledge of God. But how can it benefit us to know God's revelation of Himself, His promises, His deeds, and His guidance for living? (Optional: See Deuteronomy 4:5-8; Psalm 19:7-11.)

Law (3:19). When Paul uses the word *law* in Romans, he refers to the whole Old Testament. In 3:10-18, Paul quotes from the Psalms, Ecclesiastes, and Isaiah, not the books of Moses. He uses the word *law* flexibly, so we have to interpret him according to the context. For example, in 3:27, the NIV and RSV sometimes interpret the word *law* as "principle."

fyi

5 What responsibilities go along with being trusted with God's words?

6   What advantage did the Jews have over the Gentiles (see 3:1-2), and in the end, why did it essentially not matter?

7   Explain what Paul meant in 3:5-8.

8   What are some purposes of God's law (see 3:19-20)?

9 In view of God's righteousness, why is it impossible for us to boast about ourselves (see 3:27-28)?

live

10 In what ways do you seek praise or acceptance from people, and in what ways do you seek praise from God?

11 Do you think seeking praise only from God would affect your actions at home, school, or work? How?

connect

In your group, spend time in silence together thinking about God's equal love for all His children. Meditate on the Scriptures you just read and consider how you can learn to love like Christ. After about five minutes, talk with each other about the thoughts you had.

go deeper

By what standard will God judge people who claim to have faith in Christ? Consider some of these verses:
- Matthew 7:21-23; 25:31-46
- Luke 12:47-48
- Ephesians 4:1
- Hebrews 11:1-12
- James 2:14-26
- 1 John 1:8–2:6

memory verse of the week

Did a particular verse make you think? Is there a verse you can't get out of your head? Write it down and memorize it. Allow God's Word to permanently brand itself in your head and your heart.

notes from group discussion

you didn't earn it

Lesson 4

But God demonstrates his own love for us in this: While we were still sinners, Christ died for us.

Romans 5:8

It's not surprising that we think we can earn our way into God's good graces. After all, here on earth, we earn our way into just about everything. We earn good grades, with which we earn our way into a good college, which provides an opportunity to earn a good internship, which then gives us a foot in the workplace door to earn a good salary.

In this section of Romans, Paul makes it undeniably clear (to the Jews and to us) that God's way is simply not our way. The reason, the plain truth, is that we can't earn God's righteousness—we're too weak. Instead, it requires faith. But before Paul can convince those reading his letter that faith is what's important, he's got to prove it. He does so by addressing two of the most famous fathers in history: Abraham, the father of the Jews, and Adam, the father of humanity and sin.

Read Romans 4–5.

Our Father

fyi

But not before God (4:2). This means that if—and only if—Abraham was justified by works, then he could boast. But in God's eyes, Abraham was not justified by works but by his belief.

1 Think about a time when you tried to earn God's favor. How did it turn out?

2 In Psalm 32:1-2, David describes what God does when He credits righteousness to a person.

a How does God make a person righteous?

b What do you think it means to be blessed by God?

• *Not after, but before (4:10).* God pronounced Abraham righteous (see Genesis 15:6) about fourteen years before he was circumcised (see Genesis 17:23-24). In this one statement, Paul proves that circumcision does not make a person righteous before God; rather, it is a statement of an already existing faith.

• *Who gives life to the dead (4:17).* Abraham believed that God could bring life from Sarah's dead womb and that if he sacrificed his son Isaac in obedience to God, God would raise Isaac from the dead to fulfill His promise of descendants through him (see Genesis 22:1-19). Abraham's belief in God's promise was so strong that he was willing to kill his own son. *That's* faith.

• *Hope (5:2,4-5).* Hope does not mean a mood of wishfulness but rather something we expect with certainty. We have a sure expectation that we'll experience the "glory of God" and salvation from God's wrath.

3 Circumcision was a sign (pointer) and seal (outward guarantee) of the righteousness Abraham had by faith. What are the signs and seals of a Christian's righteousness by faith? (Optional: See John 13:35; Acts 2:41; 8:12; 10:47; Ephesians 1:13-14; 4:30; 1 Peter 3:21.)

4 God's promises are worthless if the only people who can inherit them are those who live up to them through perfect obedience (see 4:14-15). Why are they worthless in this context?

5 Romans 5:1-11 describes what is true of our lives because we've been justified and reconciled to God. Write down as many benefits of justification as you can find in those verses.

From Adam to Christ

Romans 5:12-21 lays the groundwork for our understanding of chapter 6, which discusses living in light of our union with Christ. Most of us have a really hard time grasping the key concept in this passage because it is alien to our individualistic way of thinking. Here are some keys to help:

  • Adam was a historical person, just like Jesus was.
  • The human race is a unity, a federation, like cells in a body. Adam was the head of the race. Therefore, his decision to sin affected all of us, just as a person's decisions in his head affect

the rest of his body. So, when Adam sinned, he put all of us at war with God. It doesn't seem fair, but:

- We have to deal with it. Period.
- Each one of us repeats Adam's rebellion, whether we want to or not.
- Our connectedness as a race is also what allows Christ's death to affect us.

6 With these concepts in mind, compare and contrast Adam and Christ using 5:12-21 as your guide.

fyi **Because all sinned (5:12).** There are two possible interpretations of this phrase:

1. *Each person dies because he sins.*[1] This works because it's the most obvious meaning to "all sinned." Also, Paul says God will judge each person according to his own deeds (see 2:6,12) and that everyone sins (see 1:18-32).

2. *Each person dies because he is part of the human race, all of which inherited sin when its representative, Adam, sinned.*[2] This would mean that we were born with a sinful nature because Adam, the head of the human race, sinned.

Either way you interpret the statement, most Christians agree that all people will inherit Adam's will to sin. Those who die before they get a chance to sin are just as corrupt by nature as those who live long enough to act out their sinfulness. We are not sinful because we sin; we sin because we are sinful.

7 Paul uses the phrase "how much more" to show the difference between Adam and Jesus. Why is Jesus' effect much more than Adam's (see 5:15-17)? Is there any reason why it wouldn't be?

8 What effect did God's righteous law have on mankind? Why did God want His law to have that effect (see 5:20-21; 7:13)?

live

9 How can being righteous rather than sinful before God affect your life right now?

10 With whom can you share what you have learned about Adam and Christ? Why that particular person?

connect

This section is thick with theological reasoning. If you haven't already, take as much time as you need to sort through any questions you have from this lesson. If you're a group leader, bring some study resources (see page 121 for examples) with you in case your group desires additional help.

11 In what sense do people who do not know God's law (for example, the people who lived between Adam and Moses and people today who live in places where they do not have access to the Word) still sin? (See 1:18-21,28; 2:12,14-15 for additional insight.)

12 In what sense are those people not able to sin (see 5:13-14)?

13 Why do those people die anyway?

memory verse of the week

Did a particular verse make you think? Is there a verse you can't get out of your head? Write it down and memorize it. Allow God's Word to permanently brand itself in your head and your heart.

notes from group discussion

excuses, excuses

What then? Shall we sin because we are not under law but under grace? By no means!

Romans 6:15

Being human and making excuses go hand in hand. We make excuses for everything. "I couldn't get to work on time because my car wouldn't start." Or "I'm sorry I cheated on you, but the girl was so attractive!" Or "I wasn't planning to eat four cheeseburgers, but the waitress kept bringing them, and I would have felt guilty if I'd left them on my plate." Some excuses are more ridiculous than others.

But probably the most ridiculous excuse of all is the one Paul refutes in the sixth chapter of Romans: "I kept on sinning only because I wanted God's grace to abound." And while we all know this excuse is absurd, many of us have used it at one time or another. We just modify it a little to fit our own situations: "I figured if I smoked pot, I could tell my nonbelieving friends about how God saved me from that lifestyle." The truth is, we love sinning, and we believe the lie that we are exercising freedom and actually making God look better. Knowing that we all have fallen into this trap, Paul spends this section of Scripture addressing the ideas of sin, grace, and freedom. How do they all work together?

Read Romans 6:1–7:6.

study

1 What are some basic reasons we shouldn't sin?

- *Baptized into his death (6:3).* Christ's death is the official   fyi
  atonement (translation: method of making everything okay
  between God and us) for anyone who puts his faith in Jesus, even
  before he is baptized. But although baptism does not determine
  a person's salvation, it is (1) God's public proclamation that He is
  accepting Christ's death in exchange for the consequence of the
  person's sins and (2) the believer's public proclamation that he is
  putting his faith and allegiance in Christ.[1] That's a lot of words to
  say simply this: Baptism is important.

- *Body of sin (6:6).* This refers to the old self, which was dominated
  by sin. It includes the physical, emotional, psychological, intellectual,
  and spiritual self.[2]

2 When Christ was crucified, why was death given control over
Him? (For help, see 2 Corinthians 5:21; Isaiah 53:4-6,11-12; Romans
4:25; 5:21.)

3 After Christ was raised from the dead, why did sin and death no longer have mastery over Him?

4 Paraphrasing a verse is a great way to discover if you understand it. Read the following statements and explain in your own words what happened when we were baptized into Christ's death.

We were "buried with" Christ (6:4).

We were "united with him . . . in his death" (6:5).

"Our old self was crucified with him so that the body of sin might be done away with" (6:6).

We were made "no longer . . . slaves to sin" (6:6)
and were "freed from sin" (6:7).

5 Why is it necessary to count ourselves dead to sin and alive to
God?

Not under law (6:14). This means that Christians are free
from having to deal with the condemnation and penalties
that went with God's law. Instead, Christians are judged based on the
intervention of Jesus. Apart from grace, people can try to meet God's
expectations through their own effort (and we know how easy that
is), but grace empowers believers to live up to what God desires.

fyi

6 How does Paul describe being "under grace" in 6:15-23?

7 Think about yourself and the people in your life. What benefits do people believe they gain from disobeying God and serving only themselves?

8 Why is it impossible to be our own masters—enslaved neither to God nor to sin?

9 Paul used the analogy of slavery in describing our relationship with God.

   a In what ways is our relationship with God like slavery?

   b In what ways is it not like slavery?

10 Why do you think Paul used marriage as yet another analogy for our relationship with Christ? Explain in your own words what 7:1-6 says.

> live

11 Describe some ways you've been living according to a rule, or assumed rule, instead of according to the way God's Spirit leads you.

12 Ask God to show you how to obey according to the Spirit instead of a written (or unwritten) code. Ask Him to enable you to obey joyfully rather than out of fear, guilt, or failure.

connect

Talk with your group about common excuses Christians make when deciding to sin. Get as vulnerable as you want—if you want to disclose personal stories, feel free to do so. Then pray with each other, asking God to convict you by His Spirit when you are acting out of deliberate disobedience.

go deeper

When Paul says we died to the law (see 7:4), does he mean not only that we are freed from its condemnation but also that we don't have to obey it? Should a Christian who is free from the law still obey the Ten Commandments? (See Romans 3:31; 7:12,14,25; 8:4; 13:8-10; Matthew 5:17-48.)

memory verse of the week

Did a particular verse make you think? Is there a verse you can't get out of your head? Write it down and memorize it. Allow God's Word to permanently brand itself in your head and your heart.

notes from group discussion

at war with myself

I do not understand what I do.
For what I want to do I do not
do, but what I hate I do.

Romans 7:15

"What's your New Year's resolution?"

Why do we ask that question, anyway? Perhaps it has something to do with the gorging many of us do during the Christmas season, but there seems to be more to it. Perhaps we need a new resolution every year because we rarely keep the ones we've made in previous years. We swear we will cut back on junk food or have quiet times every day or be more diligent in school. But that lasts about a month, if we're lucky, and then we're back into the same old routine. It's a vicious cycle. Over and over, we resolve to do right, and then we turn around and do exactly the things we've resolved to avoid or fail to do the things we should.

The seventh chapter of Romans is one of the most relevant chapters in all of Scripture because Paul connects to all of us in the rawest of terms. He admits the truth that he can't keep his resolutions any better than the rest of us. *Phew!* Without this chapter in Scripture, we would probably feel as if we're the worst Christians who ever lived. But Paul clears the air—even the most famous of Christians can't get it right.

Even more refreshing, we have a Savior who gets it right *for* us—a Savior who's perfectly aware of our vicious cycles, a Savior who doesn't let that stop Him from giving us abundant life.

Read Romans 7:7—8:17.

This passage of Scripture is particularly difficult to wade through because of its deep theology. *The Message* does an excellent job of leading readers through the passage. Consider reading it in *The Message* before you continue with this lesson.

1 In 7:7-11, Paul provides the basis for the conclusion he makes in 7:12. He explains what happened when he received the commandment, "Do not covet."

> **a** List the series of thoughts and actions Paul experienced.

> **b** Can you relate? How?

2 Before Paul recognized sin as sin, he coveted without resisting. In what ways did he change after he surrendered to Christ and became a slave of righteousness (see 7:14-25)?

3 In what way are Christians *not* slaves to God's law (see 6:14; 7:1-6), and in what way *are* we slaves (see 7:16,21-25)?

Not slaves

Still slaves

4 In what specific ways do you experience the struggle Paul discusses in 7:14-25? If you don't experience that struggle, why do you think that is?

fyi

Body of death (7:24). This possibly refers to the "old self," the sin nature.[1] Or it could mean life in Paul's current body, still burdened by the sinful nature.[2] Or, even still, it could mean the deadly weight of sin against which Paul struggled.[3]

5 What hope did Paul have of deliverance from his struggle against sin (see 7:24-25)? Explain this in your own words.

6 The written law of the Old Testament can't force us to obey God, bring about life, or free us from sin and death—as much as many of us would like it to since it would be so much easier (see 7:10,15-18). What has God done that the law is powerless to do (see 8:2-3)?

7 In 8:5-8, Paul contrasts life "according to the flesh" and "according to the Spirit" (NKJV). List as many contrasts as you can find.

Flesh   **Spirit**

Controlled by (8:8-9). Literally, this means "in" the flesh or "in" the Spirit. And that means to be united, directed toward, and impelled by one or the other, but not in an extreme sense that would include the loss of free will.

fyi

8 In 8:12, Paul tells us that we do not have any obligation to the sinful nature.

> **a** What do we have an obligation to? (Hint: The word *therefore* in 8:12 points backward to 8:1-11.)

> **b** Why do we have this obligation? (Hint: The word *For* in 8:13 points to the reason.)

fyi ▸ **Abba (8:15).** *Abba* is an affectionate, intimate Aramaic word for Father, comparable to Papa or Daddy. Jews never used this informal term for God, but Jesus used it and encouraged His disciples to do so too. Pretty controversial stuff.

9 Romans 8:15-16 describes what is true of us if the Spirit lives in us and leads us. Think of what this can mean for your life. What attitudes and actions would you have if you seriously considered God your Abba? (Take a look at this passage in *The Message* for another way to think about it.)

live

10 Make a list of the struggles with sin that you're currently facing (feel free to do this in your private journal). How is your flesh pulling you? How is the Spirit pulling you? Ask God to help you focus your mind on the desires of the Spirit. Thank Him that He will help you and then go and act in faith.

connect

Talk with your group about the path to holiness. Is this path a daily process or a one-time victory? Discuss the reasons for your answers. If you'd like, look up Romans 8:5-13 and Luke 9:23 for support.

go deeper

Think about how being baptized into Christ's death and united with Him in His life enables us not to sin (see Romans 6:1-14).

memory verse of the week

Did a particular verse make you think? Is there a verse you can't get out of your head? Write it down and memorize it. Allow God's Word to permanently brand itself in your head and your heart.

notes from group discussion

according to the Spirit

Lesson 7

For I am convinced that neither death nor life, neither angels nor demons, neither the present nor the future, nor any powers, neither height nor depth, nor anything else in all creation, will be able to separate us from the love of God that is in Christ Jesus our Lord.

Romans 8:38-39

Let's say you're sitting in class and you just finished the hardest test of your life. Not only was this test impossible, but it was also the deciding factor of your final grade. If you fail, you don't graduate. And let's say that you weren't able to study last night because your computer crashed, but that didn't matter much because you just found out your parents are getting a divorce, your "best friend" hates you and has been spreading rumors about you, and to top it all off, your precious goldfish, Frodo, died.

Although this may seem like a particularly huge heap of junk piled into a single day, we can relate to days like this. We go through hard times. And the pain goes deeper than just situational frustration—it forms a hurt deep within us.

In this section of Romans, Paul doesn't shy away from that truth. In fact, he hammers it down: Life is painful. But he doesn't stop there. He helps us see that pain *means* something. The pain we experience in this life creates in us an expectancy and hope for Christ's return; Paul actually calls it "birth pangs." And even more, Paul reminds us that nothing needs to faze us because Jesus loves us, and nothing can take us away from that simple and overwhelming reality.

Read Romans 8:18–9:29.

1 Make a list of everything the Spirit does or demonstrates as described in 8:11-27.

fyi

• *If indeed (8:17).* This does not mean that we suffer to attain glory; through Christ's suffering, we know that we will be in His glory no matter how much or how little we suffer. What it does mean is that just as Christ suffered and was then made glorious, so we will suffer on this earth and then experience His glory in heaven.

• *Frustration (8:20).* When Adam sinned, God announced the inevitable consequence: The ground that Adam cultivated was cursed (see Genesis 3:17-19). God's creation was meant to glorify Him, but because we messed up our lives, we can't possibly take perfect care of the world around us (and it's too late; God has already given us dominion over the earth). Therefore, the creation is frustrated because it's unable to completely fulfill its perfect purpose. But God will redeem it just as surely as He will redeem us.[1]

2 Why is sharing Christ's suffering worth the pain (see 8:17-18)?

3 Hope of glory helps us get through suffering and frustration (see 8:17-25). Another support we have is the Holy Spirit. How is He an enormous help to us?

4 How does 8:28 encourage you as you face suffering, frustration, and the struggle against sin? And don't give a cheesy or pat answer. Be real. If it doesn't help, explain that too.

fyi

• **Called (8:28).** God loved and called us not only before we became holy by receiving Christ's grace but even before we were declared righteous.

• **Foreknew (8:29).** This word is always a tough one to figure out, theologically speaking. Some people think Paul meant the kind of knowing that implies that God chose us by His grace alone when we were saved (see Genesis 18:19; Jeremiah 1:5; Amos 3:2).[2] Others think that *know* suggests the intimate knowledge of a marriage (see Genesis 4:1, NKJV; Hosea 13:5, NKJV).[3] Still others think it means God chose, before the beginning of time, "those who by faith would become His people."[4] The word predestined also comes into question with foreknowledge in mind. See Romans 9–11 and Ephesians 1:4-12.

5   To what has God predestined us? What is God's purpose in choosing us (see Romans 8:29; Ephesians 1:11-12)?

6   What assurance do the following verses give that in God's court of law, we will be found not guilty?

8:31

8:33

8:34

7 Most of Paul's fellow Jews rejected Christ and therefore faced eternal separation from God.

a How did Paul feel about this fact (see 9:2-3)?

b Have you ever felt that way about anyone in your life? If so, what did you do? What did Paul do?

• **Adoption (9:4).** God adopted the nation of Israel as His son (see Exodus 4:22-23; Jeremiah 31:9; Hosea 11:1).

• **Patriarchs (9:5).** This literally means "fathers" and refers to Abraham, Isaac, Jacob, Jacob's twelve sons, and possibly other Old Testament people, such as David (see Mark 11:10; Acts 2:29).

• **Rebekah's children (9:10).** This part of Scripture gets really sticky. Some people think it was unfair that God chose Isaac over Ishmael and Jacob over Esau. The question is all about favoritism. As far as Isaac and Ishmael are concerned, some Jews have justified this act of favoritism because Ishmael was born of a slave and Isaac was born of an intact marriage. But Paul wrote about Jacob and Esau too to show that this argument doesn't cut it (Jacob and Esau were born of the same parents within minutes of each other). The question is, why does God so unabashedly show favoritism, and how does that relate to us? If you're interested in exploring this controversy further, dig through some of the recommended study materials (see page 121). One thing that may help, though, is that the

Greek words for *loved* and *hated* are *chose* and *rejected*.[5] Esau was rejected so that his descendants could ultimately be saved through Jacob's descendant, Jesus.

8 Why is it significant that God chose Jacob before either he or Esau had done good or bad (see 9:11-12)?

9 Based on this, what do you think is God's "purpose in election" (9:11)? In other words, what is His ultimate goal in electing some of Abraham's biological children and setting others aside?

10 Does 9:6-13 suggest that God is unjust? Explain.

11 How does Romans 9:15 demonstrate God's character and will?

Hardens (9:18). A hard heart is unwilling to acknowledge that God is present, resistant to becoming vulnerable to God, and unable to hear and obey God. The Bible speaks of God hardening people's hearts and of those same people hardening their own hearts. It's the core mystery of predestination and human choice.

live

12 Are you ever tempted to say that God is unfair or uncaring in how He deals with people? If so, reflect on what you've read in this lesson's passage. How does it affect your view of God, if at all?

13 Meditate on God's sovereignty, His supreme power over the entire universe, as you wrestle with this topic. (See Ephesians 1:3-14 for additional insight.)

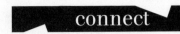

connect

Share with your group the most significant thing you learned from 9:14-29 and explain why this truth is so important to you. Pray together, thanking God for all the things He's taught you and asking for His wisdom and guidance as you try to apply these truths to your everyday lives.

go deeper

Look up the words *know* and *foreordained* in the following passages and also in a concordance. Does this help you understand the concepts of foreknowing and predestination? (Don't feel bad if it doesn't—this is a mystery that won't be solved during our time on earth. But it's well worth studying so we can have a greater respect for the complexities of such an amazing God.)

- John 10:14-15
- 1 Corinthians 8:3
- Galatians 4:9
- 2 Timothy 2:19
- 1 Peter 1:20, NKJV

memory verse of the week 🎧

Did a particular verse make you think? Is there a verse you can't get out of your head? Write it down and memorize it. Allow God's Word to permanently brand itself in your head and your heart.

notes from group discussion

God's chosen people

Lesson 8

For God has bound all men
over to disobedience so that he
may have mercy on them all.
Romans 11:32

Isn't it strange how we direct our most extreme emotions at our family members? Nobody's actions affect us more than theirs, so not only do we love them more intensely, but we also often despise them more than anyone else. Once in a while someone in a family does something so atrocious that it affects every member to the core.

We see this in Paul's frustration with his "family," Israel. Although the heart of his ministry was focused on the Gentiles, his heart was still devoted to Israel. He could relate to their problem because earlier, when he was Saul, he had been part of the problem. But finally he understood the truth of Christ and was frustrated that they didn't get it. They spent so much time reading and talking about God but completely missed the point. God was right in front of them, in Jesus, sticking out like a sore thumb amid all their flawless theology—and they couldn't see Him to save their lives.

Paul explained the state of Israel to the Roman Christians because he wanted them to understand their own position with God, whether as a Jew or a Gentile. Israel was God's chosen people, so where did Christians stand?

Read Romans 9:30–11:36.

Law of righteousness (9:31). The Old Testament law was righteous (see 7:12), and it taught the way to be right with God (see 7:12; 8:4).[1]

fyi

1 God's law described how a person could become righteous, and the Jews were correct in pursuing righteousness. However, they were going about it in the wrong way.

> **a** What was wrong with the way Israel pursued the righteousness described in the law (see 9:32)?

> **b** What was wrong with the attitude behind their zeal?

Christ is the end of the law (10:4). This comes from the Greek word *telos*, which means "termination," "fulfillment,"

fyi

or "goal." Christ is the goal and the fulfillment of the law in the sense that (1) He fulfilled all its requirements for sacrifice so we no longer have to keep the ritual laws (so if you get a skin disease, you no longer have to tell your priest who will in turn tell your whole congregation); (2) He obeyed all the law's commands (He was perfect); (3) He ended its penalties; and (4) He inaugurated the new covenant, in which we serve by the Spirit rather than by self-effort.[2]

What Paul is saying in chapter 10 is that he is frustrated with the Jews because they completely misunderstood and rejected the fact that Jesus is the goal of the law. If they had understood God's law, they would have recognized that it pointed toward and demanded a Savior who would bear man's sin.[3] They would have seen that the laws of sacrifice were meant to lead them to faith in God's mercy rather than in their ability to earn His favor by works. It just proves that none of us have a corner on understanding Scripture, but we should do our best to understand it by the power of the Spirit to avoid great misunderstandings such as this.

2 How do Moses' words in 10:5 point toward the goal and fulfillment of the law, Jesus (see 8:3-4)?

3 Read 10:9-13 in *The Message* and in another translation, such as the NIV.

a What does a Jew, or any person for that matter, need to do to be saved?

b Why are both believing and confessing important? As you think about this question, ask God to give you His wisdom so you're not just relying on what you've heard from others.

- *"Lord, who has believed our message?" (10:16).* This quote from Isaiah 53:1 is part of Isaiah's song of the Suffering Servant (see Isaiah 52:13–53:12), which describes the Servant who would bear the people's sins.

- *"Their voice has gone out" (10:18).* This reference to Psalm 19:4 testifies that the Jews couldn't blame their unbelief on a lack of opportunity to hear the "word of Christ" (10:17).

4 What does 9:30–10:21 tell us about the following?

What God does to lead someone to salvation

Our responsibility for other people's salvation

What a person must do to be saved

Actions and attitudes that keep a person from salvation

5 Summarize this passage in your own words.

---

fyi ▸ *So as to fall beyond recovery (11:11).* "Beyond recovery" is not in the original Greek, and the KJV and NASB leave it out because of that. But many commentators agree that this is what Paul actually meant.[4]

6 What good resulted from God's decision to harden most Jews (see 11:7-11)?

7 What do you think about God's decision?

• ***The part of the dough offered as firstfruits (11:16)***. Each
year, the Jews offered to God dough from their very first
grain harvest (called the firstfruits). This, in turn, made the whole
harvest holy because it then belonged to God. Paul used this analogy to show how the Jewish fathers were set apart as God's people,
which made the whole nation of Israel set apart. This didn't mean
every Jew would be declared righteous; it just meant that God
would give them some kind of blessing.[5]

• ***All Israel (11:26)***. There are three interpretations of this phrase.
Some people think this means everyone God has elected for salvation, Jews and Gentiles alike; others believe it means the total
number of elect Jews in every generation (past, present, and future);
still others think it means most Jews in the final generation before
Christ returns.[6]

8   Paul spends a lot of time in chapter 11 warning the Gentiles
about having the wrong attitude toward the Jews and their own
salvation. What is this wrong attitude, and why do you think they
would have had it? How can this relate to us?

9   What is Paul saying about Jews and Gentiles in 11:30-32?

10 How does Paul describe God in 11:33-36? Write as many observations as you can.

live

11 What responsibility do you have for another's salvation? Pray about it, asking God for wisdom. How can you act out your responsibility in someone's life this week? Ask God for opportunity and courage.

connect

In your group, discuss people or groups of people you know who have not had any opportunity to hear the good news. Make a list of these people and copy it for everyone in the group. Then commit to pray for the people on this list throughout the remainder of your Bible study. As you pray, ask God to guide your involvement in these people's lives.

How did the following people in the Old Testament pursue the law by faith rather than works, and what can you learn from them?

David (see Psalm 32; 34; 37; 40; 51)

Isaiah (see Isaiah 6:1-8; 8:11-20)

Micah (see Micah 6:6-8)

memory verse of the week

Did a particular verse make you think? Is there a verse you can't get out of your head? Write it down and memorize it. Allow God's Word to permanently brand itself in your head and your heart.

notes from group discussion

fitting in

Do not conform any longer to the pattern of this world, but be transformed by the renewing of your mind.

Romans 12:2

For most people, life in America is relatively easy. Probably too easy. There are so many conveniences, opportunities, and people. Just walk around New York City and you'll see it. Opportunities are endless, conveniences abound, and there are hoards of people everywhere you look. It's nearly impossible to stand out in the crowds because everyone is unique and no one really pays attention anyway.

So when Paul says, "Don't become so well-adjusted to your culture that you fit into it without even thinking" (Romans 12:2, MSG), what does he mean? And how can we avoid it? Paul is calling us to live a life of high standards, standards that are holy and Christlike. As you move through this lesson, think about what this means for your life and how you can avoid conforming to the patterns of the world.

Read Romans 12–13.

1 In 12:1, Paul tells us what our response to God's mercy should be. What do you think it means to:

Offer your bodies

As living sacrifices

Holy and pleasing to God

• *Do not conform any longer (12:2).* The word *conform* literally means to be molded or stamped according to a certain pattern. J. B. Phillips interprets this to mean, "Don't let the world around you squeeze you into its own mold."[1]

• *Be transformed (12:2).* The Greek verb for "be transformed" shows that this is a process; it doesn't just happen overnight.

2 According to 12:2, what needs to happen in order for us to know and agree with God's will?

3 How can we renew our minds? (Optional: See Romans 8:5,9,12-13; 2 Corinthians 3:18; Ephesians 3:14-21; 4:22-24; 5:1; 2 Timothy 3:16; Psalm 1:1-3; 119:11.)

4 Name one way in which you're tempted to conform to "the pattern of this world."

5 In 12:6-8, Paul lists examples of gifts that Christians can have. This list isn't exhaustive; it's simply meant to teach principles about how to use any gift. What principles do you think it suggests?

6 How do Paul's words in 12:3-8 affect the way you feel about your place within the body of Christ?

7 How is Christian love more than just an emotion? (See 5:6-8; 12:7-8,10-21; 13:8-10. Optional: See 1 John 3:17-18.)

- **_Do what is right in the eyes of everybody (12:17)_**. This can mean either "Do what all people, even unbelievers, know is right" or "In public, do what you know is right."

fyi

- **_Burning coals (12:20)_**. Paul is quoting Proverbs 25:21-22 here, and the statement could mean several different things. Here are two possibilities: (1) In an ancient Egyptian ritual of penance, the guilty person carried a basin of burning coals on his head as a sign of repentance;[2] or (2) the coal may depict the pain of shame. A guilty conscience is intended to drive the enemy to repent and become a friend.[3]

• **_Submit (13:1)_.** There are three other Greek words that clearly mean "obey" that could have been used here, but Paul intentionally used the word submit. It was originally a military word that meant to arrange troop divisions in marching order. To submit was to take an assigned place because it was assigned, not because of personal inferiority. The word submit includes selfless, but not blind and slavish, obedience to authority.[4]

8 Paul was not idealistic about governing authorities. The book of Acts shows that he knew all about good and bad governments. Paul knew that there would be times when, like Jesus and Peter, he would have to "obey God rather than men" (Acts 5:29). But he also knew that when he was arrested, it was crucial that he could claim to have obeyed all laws that didn't go against God's law. And he practiced what he preached. He was imprisoned, given lashings five times, and beaten three times. Why should Christians submit to governing authorities (see 13:1-5)?

9 How does Paul define the relationship between love and the Ten Commandments given in the Old Testament? (See 13:8-10; compare to 7:6,22; 8:4.)

Your neighbor (13:9). The Jews thought a neighbor was a fellow Jew, but Jesus taught that a neighbor is anyone in need, even someone we hate (see Luke 10:25-37).

fyi

live

10 Memorize 12:1-2. Make a list of ways you still conform to this world and ask the Holy Spirit to transform your mind so you can work through these things. Ask other people to pray for you and help you find Scriptures to meditate on that are relevant to your personal circumstances.

connect

If you haven't already, share with your group your answer to question 4. Talk about specific ways you can apply 12:1-2 to that temptation. Discuss what it means to conform to the patterns of this world in today's culture.

go deeper

11 Why is it wrong to repay evil with evil (see 12:14,17,19-21)?

12 How does doing good to your enemy overcome evil (see 12:20-21)?

13 If we pretend to forgive in order to make another person feel guilty, why haven't we fulfilled 12:19-21?

14 How can we be sure that our kindness to an enemy comes from sincere love?

15 How can you put 12:14,17-21 into practice in a sincerely loving and humble way this week? Ask God to give you an opportunity.

memory verse of the week

Did a particular verse make you think? Is there a verse you can't get out of your head? Write it down and memorize it. Allow God's Word to permanently brand itself in your head and your heart.

notes from group discussion

getting along

Lesson 10

Accept one another, then,
just as Christ accepted you, in
order to bring praise to God.

Romans 15:7

Even though as Christians we are members of a unified body, we still have differing opinions about God and life because we're all unique individuals within that body. Some Christians regularly appreciate a glass of cabernet, believing God is okay with the idea of drinking alcoholic beverages—and perhaps even blesses it. Others see drinking as a sin, considering it not only a dangerous endeavor (you could get drunk) but also a bad witness to nonbelievers. Some Christians believe going to church on Sunday mornings is an essential discipline of the Christian life, and others think they can find fellowship on any day outside the walls of a church building, maybe even in a bar.

Neither of these groups is right or wrong; they just have different opinions or interpretations of what it means to be a Christian. And truly, their rightness or wrongness isn't even the point. The point, rather, is that we are to love each other and glorify God. In the last section of Romans, Paul states clearly that he wants us to get along with each other, for better or for worse. He wants us to live our lives to God's glory, accepting our differences and functioning as a living, breathing, *healthy* body.

As you finish your study of Romans, think about all you've learned from this book and consider what it would be like to be a part of this body that functions with one purpose—like a well-oiled machine—to honor the God who created it.

Read Romans 14–16.

1 What reasons does Paul give for not judging other people on "disputable matters" (see 14:1-12)?

Vegetables (14:2). Most butcher shops in Paul's day were attached to pagan temples. The butchers annually sacrificed animals to their pagan gods, which is why many Christians believed it wasn't right to eat meat. Although there were Jewish butchers who didn't sacrifice their meat to idols, scholars have reason to believe many of those Jewish butchers refused to sell to Jewish Christians. So, instead of chancing unclean meat, some Christians thought it wiser to avoid meat altogether.[1] There were also some religious groups who considered meat in general unclean to eat. It was genuinely a cultural issue, as are many of our current "disputable matters."

fyi

2 If you aren't sure whether something is right or wrong, should you do it? Why or why not (see 14:14,23)?

108

Bear (15:1). This doesn't mean to just tolerate each other—to grin and bear it. Instead, it means to uphold each other lovingly.[2]

3 What might some "stumbling blocks" be for Christians today (14:13)? Why is it important to remove them if we are able (see 14:15,17-18; 15:1-3,6)?

4 Why should a Christian lovingly accept others who do something she considers foolish when Scripture doesn't specifically address the activity (see 15:7)?

5 Paul says that we are called to be unified in Christ. What does unity really mean in an everyday, getting-along-with-others sense?

6 How does Paul define his mission (see 15:15-16)?

7 In what ways can you support a missionary just as Paul wanted the Roman Christians to assist him (see 15:24,30-32)? Why is this kind of help important?

- ***Our sister Phoebe (16:1).*** Phoebe was a fellow believer. It's likely she delivered Paul's letter to the Romans because Paul started his farewells by specifically commending her to them.

fyi

- ***Priscilla and Aquila (16:3).*** This was probably a Jewish husband and wife who had worked with Paul in Corinth and were living in Rome at the time of his letter.

8 Paul closed his letter by giving praises to God. What did he say about the following?

God

The gospel (the message he wrote to the Romans and intended to preach in Spain)

live

9 What is your greatest ambition?

10 How, if at all, do you want it to mirror Paul's ambition?

connect

Talk among your group about believers you've been judgmental toward because of disputable matters. (You don't need to name names if that would be awkward.) Also, discuss ways you've been looked down on by other believers because of how you practice your freedom in Christ. Talk candidly about your reactions and learn from each other. Then pray, thanking God for making each person unique and asking Him to help you accept your brothers and sisters with love and humility.

go deeper

Think about how doing what another person thinks is wrong in his or her presence may make this person vulnerable to sin. Read chapter 14 again and ask God if there are any friends for whom you have been a stumbling block. Then listen for how God would want you to act around those friends.

memory verse of the week

Did a particular verse make you think? Is there a verse you can't get out of your head? Write it down and memorize it. Allow God's Word to permanently brand itself in your head and your heart.

notes from group discussion

review

To the only wise God be glory forever through Jesus Christ! Amen.

Romans 16:27

By now, you've got the book of Romans mastered, right? You can share the gospel flawlessly, articulating the great mysteries of God to someone who's never heard of them. And, of course, now that you've studied Romans, you'll never try to earn God's affection because you no longer struggle with insecurity, and you definitely don't struggle with sin.

Yeah, right. None of these things are true, but don't feel bad about it. (If you do, you've missed the point of the letter.) In Romans 12:2, Paul encourages us to be transformed. But transformation is a lifelong process.

Skim through the book again, paying special attention to the places you connected with most.

Read Paul's letter to the Romans.

1 In lesson 1, you listed themes you noticed during your first reading. After closer study of the letter, how would you now summarize Paul's main reasons for writing this letter?

2 What is righteousness, and how does it relate to you?

3 In your own words, write the guidelines Paul gives Christians for relating with the following people.

Other Christians (see 12:1-21; 13:8–15:13)

Government officials (see 13:1-7)

Non-Christians, including enemies (see 12:9-21; 13:8-10)

4   What are the most important truths you learned from Romans about the following?

God the Father

Jesus Christ

The Holy Spirit

live

5   Have you noticed any areas in your life (thoughts, attitudes, opinions, behaviors) that have changed because of your study of Romans? If so, what?

6 Look back over the Live sections of this study and pay attention to the applications you wanted to make. Are you satisfied with how you have followed through? Pray about any of those areas, or any new areas, you think you should continue to work on. Write your plans here.

connect

Talk with your group about your experience studying Romans together. How did you relate with each other? What did you learn from each other? How can you encourage one another? Do you want to continue with another Bible study? (If so, track down another TH1NK: LifeChange study and get to it!)

go deeper

Define these words using terms the average person can grasp. (Now that you've studied Romans, you should have a basic understanding of these words; reviewing their meanings will help you when explaining this book or the gospel to someone else.)

Sin

Grace

118

Faith

Justification

Atonement

Flesh

Spirit

memory verse of the week

Did a particular verse make you think? Is there a verse you can't get out of your head? Write it down and memorize it. Allow God's Word to permanently brand itself in your head and your heart.

notes from group discussion

study resources

It's true that studying the Bible can often lead you to answers for life's tough questions. But Bible study also prompts plenty of *new* questions. Perhaps you're intrigued by a passage and want to understand it better. Maybe you're stumped about what a particular verse or word means. Where do you go from here? Study resources can help. Research a verse's history, cultural context, and connotations. Look up unfamiliar words. Track down related Scripture passages elsewhere in the Bible. Study resources can help sharpen your knowledge of God's Word.

Below you'll find a selected bibliography of study resources. Use them to discover more, dig deeper, and ultimately grow closer to God.

historical and background sources

Carson, D. A., Douglas Moo, and Leon Morris. *An Introduction to the New Testament.* Grand Rapids, MI: Zondervan, 1992.
Provides an overview of the New Testament for students and teachers. Covers historical and biographical information and includes outlines and discussions of each book's theological importance.

Packer, James I., Merrill C. Tenney, and William White Jr. *The Bible Almanac.* Nashville: Nelson, 1980.
Contains information about people of the Bible and how they lived. Photos and illustrations help the characters come to life.

Tenney, Merrill C. *New Testament Survey.* Grand Rapids, MI: Eerdmans, 1985.
Analyzes social, political, cultural, economic, and religious backgrounds of each New Testament book.

concordances, dictionaries, and atlases

concordances

If you are studying a specific word and want to know where to find it in the Bible, use a concordance. A concordance lists every verse in the Bible in which that word shows up. An *exhaustive* concordance includes every word in a given translation (there are different concordances for different Bible translations), and an *abridged* or *complete* concordance leaves out some words, some occurrences of the words, or both. Multiple varieties exist, so choose for yourself which one you like best. *Strong's Exhaustive Concordance* and *Young's Analytical Concordance of the Bible* are the most popular.

bible dictionaries

Sometimes called a *Bible encyclopedia*, a Bible dictionary alphabetically lists articles about people, places, doctrines, important words, customs, and geography of the Bible. Here are a few to consider:

The New Strong's Expanded Dictionary of Bible Words. Nashville: Nelson, 2001.
> *Defines more than 14,000 words. In addition, it includes an index that gives meanings of the word in the original language.*

Nelson's New Illustrated Bible Dictionary. Nashville: Nelson, 1996.
> *Includes over 500 photos, maps, and pronunciation guides.*

The New Unger's Bible Dictionary. Wheaton, IL: Moody, 1988.
> *Displays pictures, maps, and illustrations. Clearly written, easy to understand, and compatible with most Bible translations.*

Vine's Expository Dictionary of New Testament Words. Peabody, MA: Hendrickson, 1993.
> *Lists major words and defines each New Testament Greek word.*

bible atlases

We often skim over mentions of specific locations in the Bible, but location is an important element to understanding the context of a passage. A Bible atlas can help you understand the geography in a book of the Bible and how it may have affected the recorded events. Here are two good choices:

The Illustrated Bible Atlas. Grand Rapids, MI: Kregel, 1999.
    Provides concise (and colorful) information on lands and cities where events took place. Includes historical notes.

The Carta Bible Atlas. Jerusalem: Carta, 2003.
    Includes analytical notes on biblical events, military campaigns, travel routes, and archeological highlights, as well as indexes. A very popular atlas for students, scholars, and clergy.

for small-group leaders

If you are the leader of a small group or would like to lead a small group, these resources may help:

Beyerlein, Ann. *Small Group Leaders' Handbook.* Downers Grove, IL: InterVarsity, 1995.
    Teaches the biblical basis and growth stages of small groups. Helps leaders develop skills for resolving conflict, leading discussion, and planning for the future.

McBride, Neal F. *How to Lead Small Groups.* Colorado Springs, CO: NavPress, 1990.
    Covers leadership skills for all kinds of small groups. Filled with step-by-step guidance and practical exercises focusing on the most important aspects of small-group leadership.

Polich, Laurie. *Help! I'm a Small-Group Leader.* Grand Rapids, MI: Zondervan, 1998.

Offers tips and solutions to help you nurture your small group and accomplish your goals. Suggests techniques and questions to use in many Bible study circumstances.

bible study methods

Fee, Gordon, and Douglas Stuart. *How to Read the Bible for All Its Worth.* Grand Rapids, MI: Zondervan, 2003.

Offers chapters on interpreting and applying the different kinds of writing in the Bible: the Epistles, the Gospels, Old Testament Law, Old Testament narrative, the prophets, psalms, wisdom literature, and Revelation. Also includes suggestions for commentaries on each book of the Bible.

LaHaye, Tim. *How to Study the Bible for Yourself.* Eugene, OR: Harvest House, 1998.

Teaches how to illuminate Scripture through study. Gives methods for understanding the Bible's major principles, promises, commands, key verses, and themes.

Wald, Oletta. *The New Joy of Discovery in Bible Study.* Minneapolis: Augsburg, 2002.

Helps students of Scripture discover how to observe all that is in a text, how to ask questions of a text, and how to use grammar and passage structure to see the writer's point. Teaches methods for independent Bible study.

notes

Lesson 2: Good News and Bad News

1. Erich von Eicken and Helgo Lindner, s.v. "Apostle," *The New International Dictionary of New Testament Theology*, vol. 1, ed. Colin Brown (Grand Rapids, MI: Zondervan, 1975), 128.
2. C. E. B. Cranfield, *Romans: A Shorter Commentary* (Grand Rapids, MI: Eerdmans, 1985), 8.

Lesson 3: The Blame Game

1. Kenneth Barker, ed., *The NIV Study Bible* (Grand Rapids, MI: Zondervan, 1985), 31.

Lesson 4: You Didn't Earn It

1. C. E. B. Cranfield, *Romans: A Shorter Commentary* (Grand Rapids, MI: Eerdmans, 1985), 113–114.
2. F. F. Bruce, *The Epistle to the Romans* (Grand Rapids, MI: Eerdmans, 1963), 129; John Murray, *The Epistle to the Romans* (Grand Rapids, MI: Eerdmans, 1959), 182–187; Charles Hodge, *Commentary of the Epistle to the Romans* (Grand Rapids, MI: Eerdmans, 1947), 148–155.

Lesson 5: Excuses, Excuses

1. C. E. B. Cranfield, *Romans: A Shorter Commentary* (Grand Rapids, MI: Eerdmans, 1985), 130–131; Kenneth Barker, ed., *The NIV Study Bible* (Grand Rapids, MI: Zondervan, 1985), 1713; F. F. Bruce, *The Epistle to the Romans* (Grand Rapids, MI: Eerdmans, 1963), 136; John Murray, *The Epistle to the Romans* (Grand Rapids, MI: Eerdmans, 1959), 214.
2. Charles Hodge, *Commentary of the Epistle to the Romans* (Grand Rapids, MI: Eerdmans, 1947), 197; Cranfield, 134; Bruce, 138–139; Barker, 1714.

Lesson 6: At War with Myself

1. Kenneth Barker, ed., *The NIV Study Bible* (Grand Rapids, MI: Zondervan, 1985), 1716.

126

2. C. E. B. Cranfield, *Romans: A Shorter Commentary* (Grand Rapids, MI: Eerdmans, 1985), 169; John Murray, *The Epistle to the Romans* (Grand Rapids, MI: Eerdmans, 1959), 268–269.
3. Charles Hodge, *Commentary of the Epistle to the Romans* (Grand Rapids, MI: Eerdmans, 1947), 238.

Lesson 7: According to the Spirit
1. C. E. B. Cranfield, *Romans: A Shorter Commentary* (Grand Rapids, MI: Eerdmans, 1985), 196; Kenneth Barker, ed., *The NIV Study Bible* (Grand Rapids, MI: Zondervan, 1985), 1717.
2. F. F. Bruce, *The Epistle to the Romans* (Grand Rapids, MI: Eerdmans, 1963), 177; Cranfield, 205; John Stott, *Men Made New: An Exposition of Romans 5–8* (Downer's Grove, IL: InterVarsity, 1966), 101; Charles Hodge, *Commentary of the Epistle to the Romans* (Grand Rapids, MI: Eerdmans, 1947), 284.
3. Stuart Olyott, *The Gospel As It Really Is: Paul's Epistle to the Romans Simply Explained* (Hertfordshire, England: Evangelical Press, 1979), 80.
4. Barker, 1718.
5. Barker, 1719; Cranfield, 229–231; Hodge, 230.

Lesson 8: God's Chosen People
1. Kenneth Barker, ed., *The NIV Study Bible* (Grand Rapids, MI: Zondervan, 1985), 1720; C. E. B. Cranfield, *Romans: A Shorter Commentary* (Grand Rapids, MI: Eerdmans, 1985), 247–250.
2. F. F. Bruce, *The Epistle to the Romans* (Grand Rapids, MI: Eerdmans, 1963), 203; Charles Hodge, *Commentary of the Epistle to the Romans* (Grand Rapids, MI: Eerdmans, 1947), 335–336.
3. Hodge, 335; Cranfield, 252–253.
4. Hodge, 361; Cranfield, 274; Martin Luther, *Commentary on Romans* (Grand Rapids, MI: Kregel, 1982), 143; F. L. Godet, *Commentary on the Epistle to the Romans* (Grand Rapids, MI: Zondervan, 1956), 399.
5. Hodge, 366–367; Barker, 1723.
6. Barker, 1724.

Lesson 9: Fitting In
1. J. B. Phillips, trans., *The New Testament in Modern English* (New York: Macmillan, 1958), 332.

2. F. F. Bruce, *The Epistle to the Romans* (Grand Rapids, MI: Eerdmans, 1963), 230; Kenneth Barker, ed., *The NIV Study Bible* (Grand Rapids, MI: Zondervan, 1985), 981–982.

3. C. E. B. Cranfield, *Romans: A Shorter Commentary* (Grand Rapids, MI: Eerdmans, 1985), 316–317; Warren W. Wiersbe, *Be Right: An Expository Study of Romans* (Wheaton, IL: Victor, 1977), 144; Bruce, 230; Stuart Olyott, *The Gospel As It Really Is: Paul's Epistle to the Romans Simply Explained* (Hertfordshire, England: Evangelical Press, 1979), 118; Charles Hodge, *Commentary of the Epistle to the Romans* (Grand Rapids, MI: Eerdmans, 1947), 402.

4. Cranfield, 320–321.

Lesson 10: Getting Along

1. C. E. B. Cranfield, *Romans: A Shorter Commentary* (Grand Rapids, MI: Eerdmans, 1985), 336.

2. Kenneth Barker, ed., *The NIV Study Bible* (Grand Rapids, MI: Zondervan, 1985), 1728.